WELCOME

TO THE UNITED STATES

A Guidebook for Refugees

Third Edition
2004

Prepared by the Center for Applied Linguistics
Cultural Orientation Resource Center
Washington, DC

Representatives from the following agencies contributed to the first two editions of *Welcome to the United States: A Guidebook for Refugees:*

African Services Committee of New York
Center for Applied Linguistics
Church World Service
International Catholic Migration Commission
International Institute of Erie, Pennsylvania
International Organization for Migration
International Rescue Committee
Iowa Department of Human Services
Jewish Family Services of Baltimore
Lutheran Social Services of Fargo, North Dakota
Lutheran Social Services of the National Capitol Area
Maryland Office of Refugee Affairs
Office of Refugee Resettlement
Refugee Services Alliance of Houston
United States Catholic Conference of Bishops
World Relief

In addition to those listed above, representatives from the following agencies contributed to the current edition of this publication:

Arlington Refugee Services, Catholic Diocese of Arlington, Virginia
Hebrew Immigrant Aid Society
Immigration and Refugee Services of America

The following organizations contributed photos:

Arizona International Refugee Consortium, Inc.
Center for Applied Linguistics
Lutheran Social Services of Fargo, North Dakota
Lutheran Social Services of the National Capital Area
PhotoDisc Inc.
SAGARTdesign

Cover by Chroma Design
Interior design & production by SAGARTdesign

Welcome to the United States: A Guidebook for Refugees gives refugees being resettled in the United States general information about what to expect and what services are available to them during their first months in the country. The guide aims to help these refugees develop realistic expectations about employment, education, health care, and other aspects of life in the United States.

The guide was written under the direction of the Bureau of Population, Refugees, and Migration, the U.S. Department of State. Federal and state officials, representatives of resettlement agencies, and recently resettled refugees contributed to its content.

Available in several languages, the guide is distributed to overseas processing entities and to refugees who have been approved for U.S. admission but have not completed their processing. It is also distributed to U.S. refugee resettlement service providers so that they will be aware of the information that their refugee clients receive before arriving in the United States.

Welcome to the United States: A Guidebook for Refugees replaces an earlier publication for refugees, *A Guide to Resettlement in the United States.*

This guide may be reproduced in its entirety. However, photos and quotes may not be used for any other publication or for any other purposes without the express consent of the donor organizations.

Contents

2

Welcome to Cultural Orientation!

This *Welcome to the United States* guidebook will help you prepare for your first few months in the United States. It tells you what to expect as you find a place to live, look for work, meet Americans, and adjust to American culture and society.

Resettlement is a long, complicated process, and this guide may not answer all of the questions you have about your own situation. If you have questions that this book does not answer, or if you do not understand something in this book, ask the staff at the processing center (JVA or OPE) or your resettlement agency. They can help you find the information you need.

About the United States

The United States is a large country with a different geographic features and types of climate. The mix of population groups and the local laws differ from community to community, and each community has its own procedures for working with newcomers. Because of this, what you have heard about the United States, even from family and friends already in the United States, may not be true for you. Staff members at your resettlement agency will help you learn about your new community and understand what to expect.

Knowing English will be important for your success in the United States. You will be able to find work if you do not speak English, but your job opportunities will be limited. Learning English will help you get a better job, understand what your children are learning in school, and make friends in your new community.

4

About Americans

Most Americans value self-reliance and hard work. They expect newcomers to get jobs as soon as possible and to take care of themselves and their families. They also expect newcomers who do not speak English to learn it as soon as they can.

Americans respect people who ask questions. They believe that asking questions shows that you are trying to learn and to understand. When you do not know how to do something, do not be afraid to ask. Most Americans will be happy to help you.

Since September, 2001, some Americans have become distrustful of those who wear non-Western clothing or seem foreign in certain ways. A few people may even express anger or suspicion. But most Americans will welcome you and want to learn about your culture. If you encounter hostility, tell the staff at your resettlement agency. They can help you know what to do.

About Resettlement

Resettlement changes your life. It is the first step to becoming a permanent resident and a citizen of the United States. Refugees who came before you say that in the United States newcomers have the chance to rebuild their lives. Starting over is not easy, but it can be done. More than two million refugees have come before you, and most have done well. With your talents, your knowledge, and your courage, you can succeed, too.

We wish you well!

6

Now that the U.S. Citizenship and Immigration Services (USCIS) has provisionally approved you for admission to the United States, only a few more steps are required before you travel. You and your family must have medical examinations and pass a security clearance. The processing center staff must send information about you to your resettlement agency in the United States. The International Organization for Migration (IOM) must arrange your travel. While you are waiting to travel, you can use the time to learn about the United States and to learn some English if possible.

Medical Examination

Medical examinations are required for all members of your family. The examinations are free, and processing center staff will make the appointments. The medical examination will

- determine if you or a member of your family have medical problems that must be treated;

- make sure that there are no communicable diseases that would make you or members of your family ineligible to travel to the United States; and,

- give your resettlement agency information on any medical conditions that may need follow-up care after you arrive in your new community.

At present, the results of the medical examination are good for 1 year, although this policy could change in the future. If you do not travel within 1 year of your medical examination, you must have another exam before leaving for the United States. For individuals with certain medical conditions, such as TB or HIV, the medical examination is currently valid for only 6 months.

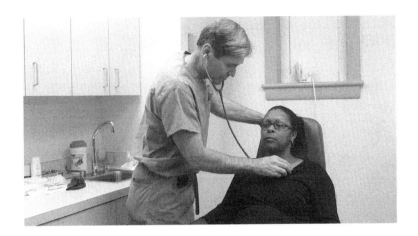

Security Clearance

All refugees must have a security clearance conducted by U.S. government authorities before they travel to the United States. Normally, this clearance is conducted before your interview with USCIS, but sometimes another security clearance is required before departure.

Sponsorship Assurance by Your Resettlement Agency

Every refugee who is accepted into the United States is assigned a resettlement agency, or sponsor, before departure. The processing center will send the following information about you to the resettlement agency:

- Your name, age, education, and occupation

- The names, ages, educations, and occupations of family members who will be coming with you

- Your ethnicity, country of origin, and religion

- Any medical problems that will need attention when you arrive in the United States

- Names, addresses, and telephone numbers of any of your relatives or friends who already live in the United States

The resettlement agency will use this information to help choose your resettlement site. If your immediate family is already in the United States, and you provide the processing center with their phone number and/or address, the agency will try to resettle you in the same town. If you ask to be resettled near a friend, or near a relative other than your spouse, child, parent, brother or sister, the resettlement agency will consider whether that area has the services you will need and whether you will be likely to find employment there. If relatives outside of your immediate family are being considered for U.S. resettlement, you may request resettlement in the same community, but there is no guarantee that this will happen.

If the resettlement agency does not have up-to-date information about your family and friends who are already in the United States, you could be resettled in a city far away from them. Give the processing center staff as much information as you can, so that the resettlement

agency will be able to choose the place that is right for you. Providing this information does not affect your immigration status or the speed of your departure. It only affects where in the United States you may be resettled. It is to your advantage to provide this information.

When your resettlement agency has decided where you will be resettled, agency staff will send this decision and their agreement to resettle you to the processing center. Before your departure, you will be told where in the United States you will be living.

Travel Arrangements and Travel Loans

The International Organization for Migration (IOM) will arrange your travel to the United States and tell you your departure date. Your family is eligible to receive a loan to pay for your transportation. Family members over 18 years of age each receive their own loan. Before you travel to the United States, you will sign a paper called a *promissory note*, promising to repay the loan. A few months after you arrive in the United States, your resettlement agency will begin sending you a bill every month for a part of the money you owe. You have 3

years to repay the whole amount. The money you repay goes into a fund that helps other refugees travel to the United States. Your repayment of this loan is the first step in your establishment of a good credit history.

If there are any changes in your family while you are waiting to travel, such as the birth of a baby, you must notify IOM or the processing center staff. Failure to do so can delay your departure.

Before you leave, IOM staff will give you an arrival package. The package contains your I-94 and customs declaration forms, medical forms and X-rays, and resettlement documents. Be careful not to lose these documents during your trip. You must carry this package of documents with you. Do not open it, and do not pack it in your suitcase. You must give the package to the immigration officials at your port of entry (the first U.S. airport at which you arrive).

Baggage

Airlines limit the size, weight, and number of pieces of baggage each person can bring. You can carry one piece, not more than 5 kg (10 lbs), on the plane with you. Each person may also bring two pieces of up to 32 kg each (70 lbs) in the plane's cargo hold. Be sure your suitcases and other bags close securely so that you will not lose anything during your trip.

Extra luggage will not be allowed on the plane. You will need to send it in advance at your own expense.

U.S. Customs does not allow some things to be carried into the United States. You may not bring in plants, fruits, vegetables, fresh meat, or drugs, for example. You may bring prescription medicine, but it must be in a container with a label. You may not carry sharp objects such as knives or scissors in your carry-on bag, but you may pack them in your checked baggage. No weapons are allowed in your carry-on baggage. If you have questions about what you can take into the United States, ask the IOM staff.

Special Travel Considerations

The trip to the United States is a long one, so you should prepare for a long journey. Traveling is tiring for everyone, and it is very difficult for young children. Have children eat something and use the toilet before they get on the plane, and bring diapers for babies. Carry packaged food for yourself and your family.

When the plane goes up and down, pressure sometimes builds up in travelers' ears. Adults and children can swallow or yawn to relieve this pressure. Plan to feed infants just after the plane takes off and just before it lands. Swallowing milk or juice will relieve the pressure in their ears.

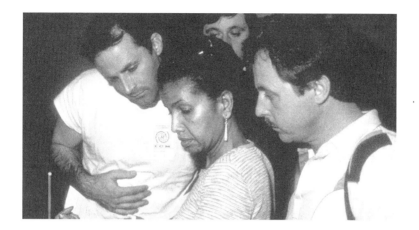

If you will need a wheelchair, crutches, or other special assistance during your trip, be sure to tell IOM. Also, if you are taking prescription medication, carry it with you so that you will have it when you need it.

If you are bringing a pet with you, you must follow U.S. Customs laws and airline regulations for transportation of animals. You must also pay the cost of the pet's transportation yourself. It is important to inform IOM if you are traveling with a pet, so that the resettlement agency in the United States can try to find housing that allows them.

Your Journey
If your travel requires you to go through several transit points before arriving in the United States, IOM representatives will assist you. In the United States, IOM representatives will meet you at the port of entry and help you with arrival procedures.

U.S. immigration officials will open your arrival package and inspect the documents. Your I-94 card will be stamped and returned to you, you will be fingerprinted, and you may receive an Employment Authorization Document (EAD) with your photo on it. Your I-94 and EAD are very important documents because they prove that you have legal refugee status in the United States. Keep them in a safe place. The resettlement agency will ask to see these documents when you arrive at your resettlement site and will make copies of them. If you notice any mistakes on these documents, please tell officials right away at the port of entry. It is easier to correct the mistake immediately than to wait until you arrive at your final resettlement site.

When you have finished with immigration procedures you will pick up your baggage and proceed to Customs. Customs officials will examine your customs declaration form and may search your bags. Once the contents of your bags have passed Customs, you will be ready for the final part of your journey.

You may have to spend the night at the port of entry because the inspections take a long time. If this happens, IOM will arrange (and pay for) a hotel room and connecting flights to your final destination the next day. When you reach your final destination airport, a relative, friend, or a representative from your resettlement agency will meet you in the baggage claim area. If for some reason there is no one there to meet you, please contact airport police right away and they will help you contact your relative or resettlement agency.

16

In the United States, the government works with resettlement agencies to resettle refugees. The government sets laws and guidelines and provides funding for the basic services that refugees receive. The resettlement agencies deliver the services and may offer additional assistance.

A resettlement agency may be a religious-based organization, a private organization, a state agency, or an ethnic organization. Although some resettlement agencies are affiliated with religious groups, you are not required to participate in their religious activities. Resettlement agencies are not allowed to encourage refugees to join any religious group.

Your resettlement agency will have a local office in or near the town where you will live, with staff who will assist you. If you have relatives living in the area, sometimes called your anchor relatives, they may help in your resettlement. Some agencies have volunteers to assist you when you arrive.

Getting Started

When you arrive, your resettlement agency will have housing ready for you. This may be long-term housing in an apartment, or it may be temporary housing with a volunteer family, with a relative, or in a hotel. If you are placed in temporary housing, the agency will help you find long-term housing as soon as possible.

The resettlement agency will pay all your basic living costs for the first 30 days after you arrive. Some agencies will pay the expenses directly. Others will give the money to you or to your relative, and you will pay the expenses yourself.

Getting Settled

The resettlement agency will advise you for the first 3 months after you arrive.

Resettlement workers, aided by relatives, friends, and volunteers, will help you find your way around your new community. With their help, you will do the following things:

- Find long-term housing
- Obtain clothing and furniture
- Learn about possible reunification with family members who are still overseas
- Get a Social Security card (you must have one to get a job)
- Look for a job
- Enroll your children in school
- Learn about the U.S. monetary system
- Learn to use public transportation
- Arrange for a medical examination and any necessary medical care
- Find English language classes
- Begin to learn about U.S. customs and laws
- Learn about community services that can help you

You will need to make good use of the services that the resettlement agency provides, because it will only provide them for the first 90 days after you arrive. After the first 90 days, available services vary depending on individual needs and your resettlement agency. You may be referred to other agencies to meet specific needs.

The resettlement agency will not pay your bills or debts. You will need to work to earn money to pay your own expenses.

The staff at your resettlement agency will be able to help you best if you work with them. Tell them about your progress, be honest about your wishes and concerns, and try to be flexible.

Moving to Another City

If you consider moving to another community, remember that your resettlement agency is not responsible for moving you, and the resettlement agency in the area you move to is not required to help you. If you decide to move, you will be responsible for your own support. If you have a question about moving, talk to the staff at your resettlement agency.

20

In addition to your resettlement agency, there are other service agencies in your community. Some are agencies of the local, state, or federal government; others are voluntary organizations, such as those affiliated with churches, mosques, or synagogues. These are called social or community service organizations.

Refugees are eligible for social services such as cash assistance and employment counseling, but the services and their availability vary from place to place. Your resettlement agency will help you learn about the services available in your local community and find out if you are eligible and how to apply.

Social service organizations provide temporary assistance to help you become self-sufficient. Service organizations determine your need by looking at how much income you earn, where you live, your age, and other factors. When your circumstances improve, the agency reduces services or stops providing them. If your situation becomes more difficult, you may become eligible for services again for a while. It is important to remember that these services are temporary; they continue only until you can support yourself.

Community services include private assistance, government assistance, and public services.

Private Assistance

Private assistance organizations provide a variety of services. The amount and type of these services vary from place to place, but many communities offer the following:

- Counseling

- Immigration status assistance

- English as a Second Language (ESL) classes

- Employment help (job counseling and vocational training)

- Translation services

One type of private assistance organization that exists in many communities is the mutual assistance association, or MAA. These are organizations formed by former refugees and immigrants to help refugees who are new to the community. MAAs may provide services such as community orientation, translation, employment assistance, transportation, and English language classes for refugees and immigrants.

Religious institutions such as churches, mosques, and synagogues may also offer various services. Some have ESL classes for adults or after school classes for children, and some distribute used clothing and furniture. Others offer programs for the elderly.

Government Assistance

Government social service agencies provide various services to the community. They help people with special needs, such as low-income families, the homeless, and people with disabilities. Refugees are eligible for several of the government assistance programs. These programs are usually administered by a government social services office, but may be administered by a private, voluntary organization, including a resettlement agency.

Government programs have strict time limits and guidelines for participation. In order to participate, applicants must fill out forms that show proof of income and other personal information. Your resettlement agency can help you find out about these programs and know whether you qualify and how to apply.

Here are the main government programs that help refugees:

Cash assistance programs. For people who are having difficulty finding a job, two programs provide temporary financial assistance: Temporary Assistance to Needy Families (TANF), for parents with dependent children, and Refugee Cash Assistance (RCA), for single and married refugees without dependent children. These programs may have different names at the local level and may differ in several ways from community to community. To qualify for cash assistance, participants must usually be in a job training program or they must show that they are looking for work. Cash assistance is only available for a few months.

Matching grant program. Many resettlement agencies offer this program instead of cash assistance for refugees who want to work but need some financial help first. Refugees who enroll in this program promise to get a job as soon as possible. In exchange, they receive increased financial assistance and job counseling, and placement services for their first 4 months in the United States.

Food stamps. This is a federal program that provides food assistance to low-income people in the United States. Refugees may apply for food stamps at a local government office. The amount of food assistance is based on family size and income. Food stamps are issued in the form of a plastic card and can be used only to purchase food items. Nonfood items such as cigarettes, alcoholic beverages, diapers, paper products, and soap cannot be purchased with food stamps.

Another federal food assistance program, Women, Infants, and Children (WIC), is available to women who are pregnant or have recently had a baby, and to infants and children up to 5 years of age. WIC provides food supplements and health education.

Supplemental Security Income (SSI). This is a federal cash assistance program for people who are blind, disabled, or over age 65. Refugees who are eligible may apply at the local Social Security office. This is the same office that issues Social Security cards.

Energy assistance. This is a federal program that helps people with low incomes pay their home heating and air conditioning expenses. Refugees can apply for energy assistance at a local government office. This program is not available everywhere.

Child care assistance programs. Some communities provide free or low-cost day care for low-income people. These programs are usually funded by the federal government and are administered by a local government office or center, such as a day care center. Parents who need child care in order to work or look for work may be eligible for this kind of assistance.

Public Services

Every community has public services available to all community members. Knowing about these services will help you use available resources and adjust to life in the United States. Here are a few of the most important public services:

Police. The police enforce the law and ensure public safety. They also respond to medical emergencies, help people who are lost, and work in inner city neighborhoods to improve community relations. You may see police officers on patrol in your community, either in cars or on foot. You should have respect for police officers' authority, but not be afraid of them. If a police officer approaches you and asks you to stop, do so. Running away will be understood as a sign that you have done something wrong and may lead to greater problems. Do not offer money to a police officer; doing so is illegal and can result in severe penalties. If you cannot communicate with the police, ask for an interpreter or contact your resettlement agency.

Emergency services. All communities have fire departments and emergency medical services. To get help in an emergency, dial 911 on the telephone. An operator will answer. Be prepared to tell the operator what you need ("Police," "Fire," or "Ambulance," for medical emergencies) and your location. If you cannot explain the problem in English, just say, "Help" or "Emergency" and do not hang up the telephone. The open phone line will help the operator know where you are.

Libraries. Many communities have public libraries that have books, magazines, and information about the community. Most libraries also have a special section and activities for children. If you get a library card, you can borrow books from the library for a few weeks. You must return the book on time, or pay a fine when it is overdue.

Parks and recreation. Local parks provide picnic areas, playgrounds, and sports fields. Your local parks and recreation department may also sponsor free or low-cost activities, such as play groups for children, sports teams, and activities for the elderly. In addition, state and national parks offer space for recreation and the enjoyment of mountains, forests, lakes, rivers, and beaches. Many parks have regulations about the kinds of activities permitted. Some parks are free, but others charge an admission fee.

You can find information about other community services in the chapters on Education and Health.

When you first arrive in the United States, your resettlement agency will have a place ready for you to stay. The place will have furniture and basic supplies. At first, you may stay with relatives who have already settled in the United States or with volunteers. Or you may be placed in an apartment, in a hotel, or in an agency welcome center. If you are single, you may be placed with other single refugees temporarily.

The resettlement agency must make sure that you have housing for your first month in the United States. If you have relatives in the United States, they may be asked to make housing arrangements for you.

Finding Housing

The staff at the resettlement agency will discuss long-term housing with you soon after you arrive. Your search for housing may take several weeks because finding a suitable place to live can be difficult. You will want to find a place that is affordable, safe, and near stores, public transportation, your workplace, and your children's schools.

To find a place to live, here are some of the things you can do:

- Talk with staff at the resettlement agency

- Get advice from your family and friends

- Get advice from people you work with

- Look for "For Rent" signs on or near buildings

- Look in the classified section of the daily newspaper

- Read special newspapers and magazines that list apartments and houses for rent

- Visit rental offices in apartment buildings

- Search on the Internet for apartments for rent

Types of Housing

Most American communities have several types of housing:

- Apartment buildings
- Single family houses
- Trailer homes
- Rooms in a house or apartment

A rental apartment usually has a kitchen with stove, sink, and refrigerator; a living and dining area; one or more bedrooms; a bathroom; and closets. The smallest kind of apartment, called a studio, has just one room with a separate bathroom and kitchen area.

Housing Costs and Safety

The cost of housing differs from state to state, from city to city, and between communities within one area. Wherever you live, however, housing costs will be the largest part of your monthly expenses.

Apartments that you can afford may only be available in low-income neighborhoods, where the crime rate is often higher than in other neighborhoods. No matter where you live, always lock your home when you leave and know which neighborhoods to avoid at night. Get to know your local police officers so that you can talk with them about crime prevention efforts in your neighborhood.

You should expect to live in a neighborhood that is racially and ethnically mixed. Your neighbors will probably be from many different nationalities and backgrounds.

“ *For us it was such a beautiful apartment, full of things we had never seen before.*

...Today I know that the people who live in this neighborhood are very poor. The apartments are small and boxy.

But together, my children and I scrubbed the walls of the apartment until they glowed in the weak sunlight, and we basked in the comfort of our new home. ”

Leases and Housing Laws

When you rent an apartment or house, you must sign a rental agreement or lease. This is a legal paper that protects both the tenant (you) and the landlord (the owner of the building). A lease protects you from unfair treatment by your landlord.

The lease states the amount of the monthly rent for the apartment or house. The rent may include the cost of utilities (electricity, gas or oil for heat, water, and trash removal), or the utilities may be charged separately. Before you sign a lease, it is important to ask the landlord if utilities are included in the rent.

When you sign a lease, you agree to the following:

- The number of people who will live in the apartment or house

- The amount of the monthly rent

- The day of the month when the rent is due

- The condition of the apartment (it will be kept clean and undamaged)

- The number of months you will stay (usually 12 months)

- The terms for moving to another apartment before the lease ends

You may be required to prove that the rent will be paid. If you are not working, you have no credit history to prove that you have a good record of paying your bills.

For this reason, you may need to find a cosigner, some-one with a good credit history who will sign the lease with you.

Tenants are usually required to pay a security deposit when they sign a lease. The security deposit usually equals 1 month's rent and is returned to you when you leave the apartment if you have fulfilled the terms of your lease.

If you break the agreements in the lease, you can be evicted (required to leave your apartment) and lose your security deposit. For example, states and cities often have housing codes that limit the number of people who can live in a given space. This means that if you have a large family, you may have to rent more than one apartment. Your resettlement agency will do its best to find two or more apartments close together.

If you have more people than the law allows living in one apartment, you can be evicted.

Housing laws apply to both landlords and tenants. Landlords must see to it that their housing meets certain standards of safety and sanitation for rental property. The landlord must be sure that electrical, plumbing, and heating systems conform to the law, and they must pro-vide smoke detectors and keep the property free of rodents and insects. Housing laws also state that land-lords cannot refuse to rent to people because of their ethnicity, religion, or country of origin.

When you first arrive in the United States, you will spend a lot of time walking from place to place. Soon you will start taking public transportation, and someday you will probably own and drive a car.

If you learn the meaning of traffic signs and signals and other rules of the road in the beginning, you will have an easier time using public transportation and learning to drive in the United States.

Public Transportation

Public transportation varies from community to community in the United States. Cities have buses, subways, and commuter trains that allow people to travel throughout the city without a car. Taxis are also available, but are usually expensive. In other areas, public transportation is not easily available. Your resettlement agency will give you detailed information about public transportation in your new community soon after you arrive.

Owning and Driving a Car

In areas where public transportation is not available or convenient, you may want to get your own car as soon as possible. Car ownership is convenient, but it is also expensive. Also, there are many responsibilities in owning and driving a car in the United States.

The laws governing car owners and drivers are set by state governments. Your resettlement agency can tell you the laws for the state you live in and give you information about where to get a permit so you can learn to drive in the United States.

To drive a car legally, you must have a local driver's license. An international driver's license is not acceptable as a substitute. If you drive without a license, you can be

charged a fine or put in prison. You have to be a certain age to drive a car; the age varies from state to state.

To get a license, you must go to the local Department of Motor Vehicles (DMV) and pass a vision test, a written test on driving laws and regulations, and a driving test. You will have to pay a fee when you apply for a license. Your driver's license will have your photo, name, address, and date of birth, and it must be renewed every few years.

Breaking certain laws may result in losing your license. For example, if you are arrested for driving under the influence of alcohol, you may lose your driver's license, pay a large fine, or spend time in jail. You might even be deported back to your home country.

After you buy a car, you must register it with the local DMV and have it inspected to be sure it is safe. You must also have insurance on your car. Insurance is provided by private insurance companies. The cost of insurance depends on where you live, how old you are, how many people will be driving the car, and your driving record. You will also need to consider the costs of gas, car maintenance, and parking.

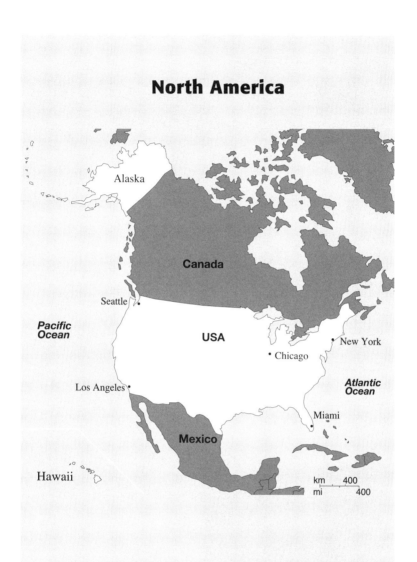

North America

New York —▶ Los Angeles (2,911 Miles/4,684 Kilometers)
New York —▶ Chicago (818 Miles/1,316 Kilometers)
New York —▶ Miami (1,325 Miles/2,132 Kilometers

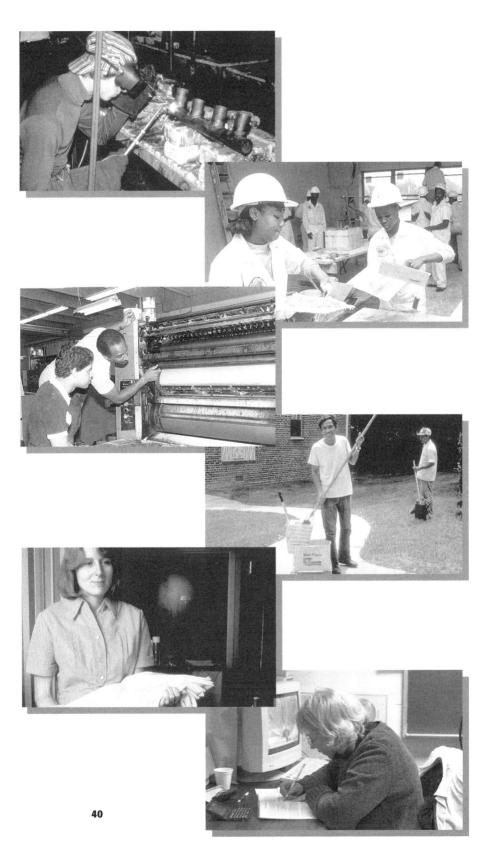

40

Most Americans place great value on being self-sufficient. They believe that adults should work to support themselves and their families, and should not rely on cash assistance from the government. For this reason, finding work is an important priority for refugees during their first few months in the United States, and one of your first goals will be to find a job.

In the beginning, you will be expected to take the first job that is offered to you, even if it is not highly paid or in your former occupation. Most Americans believe that having any job is better than having no job.

Employment is not guaranteed by the government or your resettlement agency. Refugee employment services will help you in your job search, but you will not find a job if you do not work at finding one yourself. You will be competing with others for the same jobs, so you need to show that you are ready to go to work.

Types of Jobs

In the United States, there are three general types of employment: unskilled jobs, skilled jobs, and professional jobs. For each type of job, a person needs to have a different level of experience or training.

Unskilled labor or entry-level jobs require little training or experience. Examples of entry-level jobs are hotel housekeeper, restaurant server, and factory worker. These positions usually pay an hourly wage and do not require a high level of English. Many refugees work in these jobs while studying English or learning other skills.

Skilled labor jobs require training, a higher level of

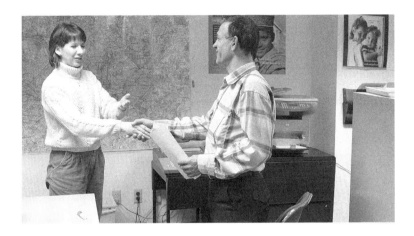

English, and a certain level of skills in the field. Mechanic, beautician, electrician, and computer technician are examples of skilled labor jobs. Skilled jobs pay an hourly or weekly wage that is higher than the wage for most entry-level jobs, and even higher than for some professional jobs. Many skilled jobs require licensing or membership in a union. Licenses from your homeland may not be accepted, but you can study English and take courses to receive U.S. certification in your field.

Professional jobs usually require at least a college degree, advanced English, and a high level of skills in the field. These skills take a long time to obtain. Many professional jobs, such as medicine or teaching, also require a license or certification for the state in which you work. Even if you are licensed in your own country, additional study and recertification tests will be required before you can practice in the United States. Most professional jobs are salaried, which means that the pay is a fixed annual amount, rather than an hourly wage.

Women and Men at Work

Both men and women work in the United States. Women make up half the work force, do the same jobs as men at all levels, and often supervise male workers. This may differ from the practice in your homeland, and you may not be used to the idea of women working outside of the home. However, there is a big advantage when both parents work, because having two incomes helps the family progress more quickly toward financial self-sufficiency. Children over the age of 15 may also work part time, and many young people in the United States work part time after school, on the weekends, and during vacations.

Looking for a Job

Your own initiative and perseverance are your best tools for finding a job. However, there are other services to support you in your efforts.

Resettlement agencies and refugee employment services. Staff at resettlement agencies and refugee employment services have helped many refugees find their first jobs in the United States. Discuss your ideas with them, and listen to their advice. They will help you understand what type of job you can expect to find with your skills and experience.

Public employment agencies. Every state has public employment agencies that can help you without charging a fee. Your resettlement agency can tell you where those offices are located.

Friends and relatives. Friends, relatives, and members of the refugee community who arrived before you can tell you about job vacancies where they work or at other businesses they know about.

Most newspapers in the United States have "Help Wanted" or "Employment" sections which list job openings.

Newspapers. Most newspapers list job openings in a help wanted section.

Private employment agencies. Private employment agencies charge a fee for helping you find a job. Some of these fees are quite high, and you should be certain that you understand their policies before signing a contract. If you do not understand, ask your resettlement agency for assistance.

Child Care

If you are a single parent, or if both you and your spouse will be working, you will need to arrange for someone to care for your children while you are at work. In some refugee families, an older relative who is not working cares for the children, or parents get jobs with different schedules so that one parent is always at home.

Most communities provide child care services, but usually there is a fee. Private individuals can also provide child care in their homes. The staff at your resettlement

44

You will be required to show proof that you are authorized to work. Most refugees use the I-94 (which has been stamped by CIS for employment authorization), a Social Security card, and a photo ID (such as an Employment Authorization Document (EAD), passport, or driver's license). You should always carry the originals of these documents to a job interview; a photocopy is not acceptable.

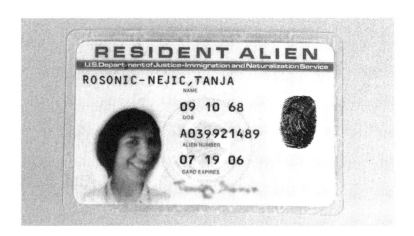

agency can advise you about child care services in your community.

Tips for Success in Job Interviews

Once you have identified possible employers, you must have a job interview. The interviewer will tell you about the work and talk with you to find out whether you will be a good worker. Here are things you can do to make a good impression:

Arrive on time. Clock time is very important to Americans. If you are late for the interview, the supervisor will think that you will also be late for work everyday.

Be clean and appropriately dressed. Your employment counselor can help you know what kind of clothing to wear.

Look the supervisor in the eye, smile, and shake hands. In some countries eye contact with a supervisor is considered rude, but Americans believe that eye contact indicates honesty, and a smile and handshake indicate a good attitude about work.

Ask questions about what you will do on the job. This shows the supervisor that you are interested.

Try to relax. Everyone is nervous in job interviews. Know that you are not the only one.

You may have to go to several interviews before you are hired. This is normal for all job seekers in the United States. You may feel discouraged if you are not hired after your first interview, but try to be patient. Ask your

family and your employment counselor for encouragement if you need it.

Pay, Withholding, Deductions, and Benefits

When offering you a job, the employer will tell you how much the pay will be, whether you will be paid an hourly wage or an annual salary, what benefits are available, how often you will be paid, how many hours per week you are expected to work, and what the work schedule is. If you don't understand something, ask about it.

You will receive your pay on a regular schedule, which may be once a week, once every 2 weeks, or once a month. You will receive your pay as a paycheck with a pay stub or statement. The pay stub is for your records; keep it when you cash or deposit the check.

The pay stub will show your gross pay, your withholding and deductions, and your net pay.

Gross pay is the total amount you earned for that pay period. It should be the number of regular hours you worked multiplied by your hourly wage.

Taxes will be taken out of your paycheck by your employer before he or she gives you your check. These taxes that have been taken out of your check are called *withholding*. When you start your job, your employer will ask you to fill out a form that reports your earnings to the U.S. Internal Revenue Service (IRS), the government agency that collects taxes. The form tells the employer how much your withholding should be. Withholding is required by law. It includes Social Security and Medicare tax (sometimes called FICA), federal income tax, and, in some states, state income tax. Each of these amounts is shown on the pay stub.

Deductions are other amounts that are taken out of your gross pay. You choose what deductions will be taken on the basis of your needs and what your employer offers. Employees often use deductions to pay for health insurance, union dues, life insurance, or a company retirement plan.

Net pay is the final amount of your paycheck after all withholding and deductions.

The pay system in the United States can be very confusing. If there is something about your paycheck or pay stub that you do not understand, ask your employment counselor or the staff at your resettlement agency for help.

In addition to your pay, your employer may provide benefits such as health insurance. Some employers provide health insurance at no cost to employees; others have employees pay part of the cost through deductions. At

some companies, the health insurance benefit becomes available to employees after they have worked for a period of time, such as 3 or 6 months.

Health costs can be quite high in the United States, so health insurance is an important benefit to consider when you are looking for a job. It may be wiser to take a lower paying job with health insurance than a higher paying job without it.

Your employer may offer additional benefits such as paid sick leave, vacation time, or retirement plans. Company policies on benefits differ greatly, so ask about them to be sure you understand what your employer offers. In some cases, benefits increase the longer you work for the company.

Three other work-related benefits are provided by law.

Social Security is a federal government program that supports retired people. The amount paid to a person is based on that person's U.S. wage history. Social

Security benefits are available only to workers who have contributed through withholding for 10 years or more.

Unemployment insurance is a state government program that provides benefits to people who lose their jobs through reasons outside their control, such as the closing of the company.

Workers' compensation provides some salary and medical coverage for workers injured on the job. Workers' compensation programs are administered by state governments.

Jobs That Pay in Cash

Working for cash is against the law in the United States because it usually means you are not paying taxes. If your employer pays you in cash, and does not give you a pay stub showing gross pay, withholding, and net pay, both you and the employer are breaking the law.

When you pay taxes, you make yourself eligible for benefits such as Social Security, workers' compensation, and

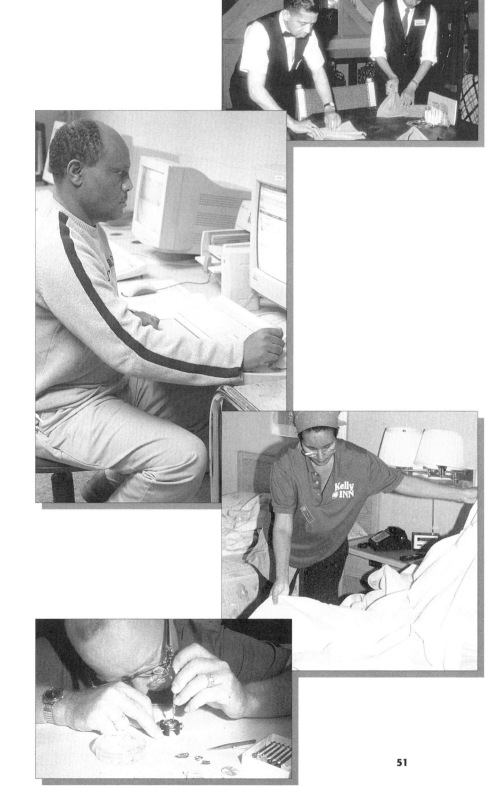

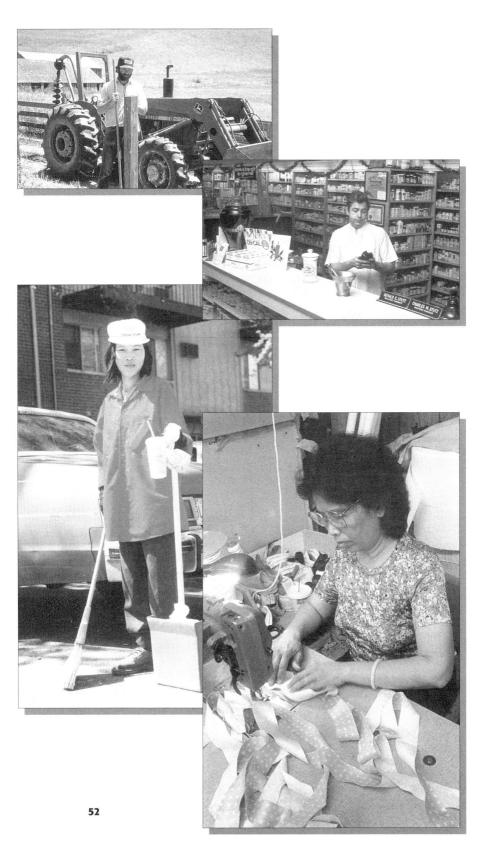

52

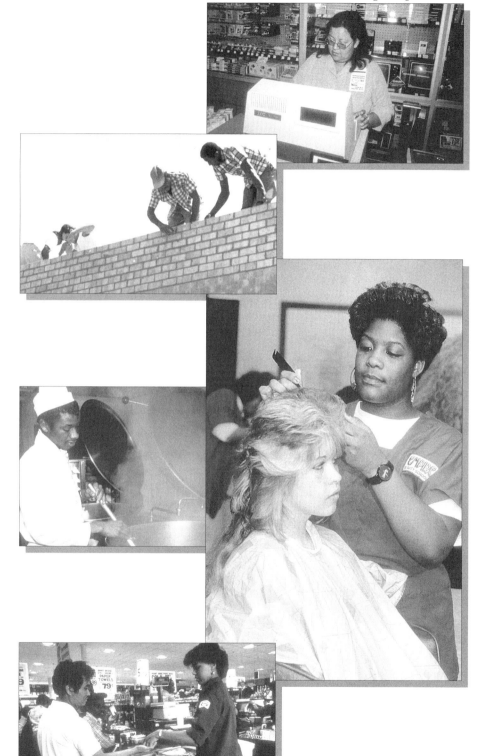

unemployment benefits. When you earn money and do not pay taxes, you are guilty of tax evasion. If you are caught, you may have to pay a fine or go to prison. You may also be deported.

Workplace Rights

As a refugee, you have the same workplace rights as an American citizen. An employer may not discriminate against you because of your refugee status or deny you a job or a promotion because of your age, color, handicap, marital status, ethnic or national origin, race, religion, or sex. However, some jobs are only open to U.S. citizens, such as most jobs with the federal government. Employment laws also protect workers from unsafe working conditions and sexual harassment in the workplace.

Employment History and Employment Goals

Your first job will be an important step in establishing a work history in the United States. You should try to stay on your first job at least 6 months, even if the job is not as professionally satisfying as you would like, because future employers will look at your performance on that job when they consider hiring you.

You should also set employment goals for yourself and identify what you will need to do to achieve them. To move up to a better, higher-paying job, you will need to improve your English and you may need to learn new skills. To return to your former profession, you may need to attend classes and obtain a certification. Your employment counselor can help you develop a plan for achieving your goals.

You will probably have to work at several different jobs before you reach your final goal. This is not unusual in the United States; many Americans change jobs several times during their working years. Achieving your goals may take time, and you will need to be patient. Above all, remember that the United States is known as a land of opportunity for those who work hard.

Tips for Success on the Job

Resettlement agencies and many refugees say that these tips can help you keep your first job and find better jobs in the future.

Be on time for work. Employers value punctuality, and you will make a good impression if you are always on time. If you arrive late to work, your pay may be reduced.

Take time off for illness only if you are very sick. Most Americans continue working if they have a minor illness, and many are proud that they have never missed a day at work because of illness.

Call if you are going to miss work. Always call your supervisor if you are going to be late or absent for any reason.

Be friendly. Lunch hour and break times can be good times to socialize with coworkers. Casual conversation topics in the United States include the weather, weekend activities, food, and sports. There will also be many opportunities to share your culture with your coworkers, especially around traditional holiday periods.

Be productive at work. Avoid personal conversations with family, friends, and coworkers and phone calls during work time.

Ask questions. If you do not understand something, ask about it. You will do a better job and your employer will respect you for trying to learn and improve.

Learn new tasks and responsibilities whenever you can. You may be able to move up to a better job if you show you are willing to assume additional responsibilities.

Give notice when you quit. When you leave one job to take another one, give your old employer at least 2 weeks' notice. Never quit a job before finding a new one.

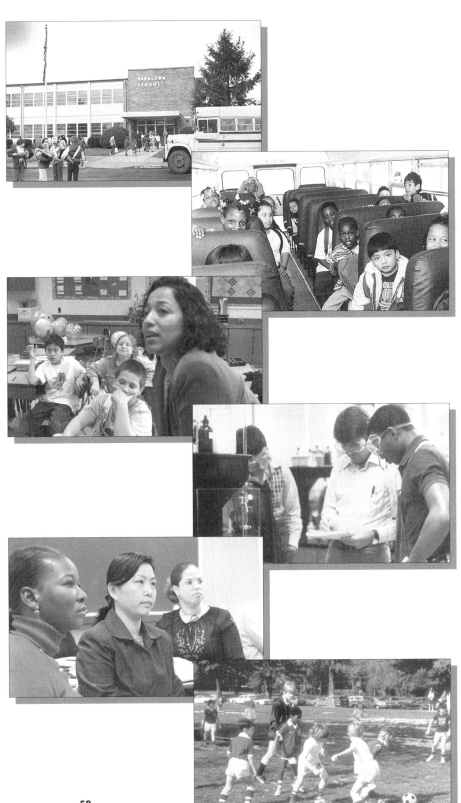

58

In the United States, education is available to everyone, regardless of age, race, religion, or social class. Most Americans view education as a way to qualify for more satisfying jobs and improve their standard of living.

Public Education for Children

Public education is free and is required by law for all children ages 6 to 16. Free public education is usually available for children ages 5 to 18, depending on local school district regulations. Parents may also enroll children in private schools, but tuition at these schools is often expensive.

In American public schools, children from different racial, religious, and socioeconomic backgrounds study and interact together in classrooms and during out-of-class activities. Boys and girls are taught together in the same classroom in almost all public schools. Children with physical or mental disabilities must also attend school. In these cases, the school assesses the child's disability and discusses with the parents a plan for the child's education.

There are three levels of education in the United States. The grades that are included in each level vary by school district.

Primary school begins with kindergarten (age 5) and continues through grade 5 or grade 6 (age 12)

Middle school or junior high school usually includes grades 6 to 8

Senior high school usually includes grades 9 to 12, through age 18. Students who successfully finish high school receive a high school diploma.

At each level, the school year begins in late August or early September and ends in late May or June. Most children attend classes about 6 hours a day, Monday through Friday. Students who need to catch up academically may have to attend summer school in June and July.

Children should be enrolled in school as soon as possible after arrival. Your resettlement agency will help you enroll your children. They will be placed in a grade on the basis of their age and previous school experience, although younger children who speak little English may be placed in a lower grade at first.

Schools require copies of the child's immunization records and medical histories. If you do not have these, or if your child has not been immunized, your resettlement agency can help arrange immunizations.

School attendance is very important. When students miss school, parents are expected to provide a written explanation, and students are expected to make up the school work they missed.

Although public education is free, parents pay some expenses, such as the costs of school supplies and fees for special activities. If the school is too far from your home for your child to walk, school buses may provide free transportation to school. Children can take lunch to school or buy low-cost, nutritious lunches in the school cafeteria.

There is no national curriculum in the United States; each state and local school district decides what should be taught. In general, most students study English, mathematics, social studies, science, and physical education. Art, music, and foreign languages are also usually offered. Most schools, particularly at the high school level, also offer sports and club activities during and after school hours.

The American teaching style may be very different from the style in your home country. Teachers encourage children to learn by thinking and analyzing more than through rote memorization. Students participate by asking questions and joining in discussions and activities, even if they do not yet speak much English.

One of the biggest challenges for children is learning English. Young children learn quite quickly, but it will take longer for older children. Many schools have special English as a second language (ESL) classes for new arrivals; others offer assistance through a special teacher or a tutor. Most newcomers face adjustment problems in their first year of school. Children may feel lonely at first, but as their ability to communicate improves, they make friends and feel more comfortable at school.

Many newcomer students and their parents are surprised by the informal behavior and dress of American students. American public schools give students freedom to make choices, but they are also expected to obey school rules. If they break the rules, students may have to do additional homework or stay after school, be denied permission to participate in certain activities, or be suspended from school for a few days. Physical punishment is not permitted in U.S. schools.

Some schools, particularly large ones in big cities, have problems with youth gangs and fighting between racial or ethnic groups. In some areas, there have also been

problems with students using drugs and bringing weapons to school. If your children feel threatened or confused, they should avoid confrontation and talk to a teacher, school counselor, or tutor.

Educators in the United States believe that parents should be involved in their children's education because this helps the children succeed in school. Schools try to help parents understand their children's education, and many offer information specifically for parents who do not speak English. At least twice a year, the school will ask you to meet with teachers to discuss your children's progress. However, you can ask to meet with your children's teachers anytime you have questions or concerns. You can also attend school meetings, even if you do not speak much English.

Education for Adults

Most Americans view education as a lifelong process, and many enroll in courses at some time during their adult lives. After deciding to continue their education, most adults continue working full time and attend courses in the evening or on the weekend.

Refugees, too, can continue their education while working. Your resettlement agency can help you find education opportunities in your community, from English as a second language (ESL) classes and high school diploma study to vocational and professional training. Once you are settled into the community, you will learn more about the educational opportunities available. You will probably have little opportunity for higher education during your first year in the United States. But later on you may decide to work on an advanced degree or professional certification. It is important for families to work together to plan how to obtain and finance education for adults in the family.

Here a few of the opportunities for education that you may find in your community:

ESL and literacy classes. Most communities offer English classes through adult education programs at community colleges and high schools. These classes are open to everyone, although some may charge a small fee. Some private, nonprofit organizations, such as resettlement agencies and MAAs, also offer ESL

classes. These are usually free, but may have long waiting lists for admission. Commercial language schools also offer English classes, but these are usually expensive. Studying with a volunteer tutor is another way to learn English, and can also be a good way to learn about American culture and customs.

In ESL classes, men and women of different ages, education, and ethnic backgrounds attend ESL classes together. In beginning-level ESL classes, students usually study the English they need to function in the community and at the workplace. In higher level classes, students pay more attention to English grammar, reading, and writing.

In literacy classes, students learn the basics of reading and writing in addition to spoken English. Because literacy is so important in American life, literacy classes are usually available at many of the same places that offer ESL classes and other types of adult education. Your resettlement agency can give you the necessary information.

Other adult education classes. Adult education programs also offer many different classes for the general public. Typical subjects include bookkeeping and accounting, secretarial skills, computer skills, and foreign languages. These classes are usually not designed for students with limited English, and participants must pay a fee.

General Educational Development (GED) diplomas. In order to advance beyond most entry-level jobs, adults usually need a high school diploma. Refugees over the age of 21 who have not had secondary education in their homelands or who do not have diplomas can study for a GED diploma. This diploma is generally accepted as the equivalent of a high school diploma. Your resettlement agency can give you information about these programs.

Vocational and technical schools. Vocational and technical schools train people for specific skilled occupations, such as auto mechanics, computer programming, and medical and dental assisting. Usually these programs require a high level of English and payment of a tuition fee. For certain skilled trades, such as plumber and electrician, on-the-job training in an apprenticeship program is required for certification.

Colleges and universities. There are two major types of higher education in the United States: community colleges and 4-year colleges and universities.

Community colleges offer 2-year programs that prepare students for certain professions, such as accounting or nursing. In some professions, students can become certified at the end of a 2-year community college program. In others, they begin in a 2-year community college program and then transfer to a 4-year program at a university. Community colleges also grant degrees in humanities, social science, and science subjects.

In 4-year colleges and universities, students are usually required to complete a general curriculum before specializing in a field such as physics, mathematics, or history, or in preparation for advanced study in law or medicine. These institutions require very high levels of English proficiency and require nonnative speakers of English to pass a language test before enrolling. Higher education is not free and can be very expensive. Most institutions have a financial aid office that provides information about student loans and scholarships. However, full scholarships are very rare, so in order to attend university you must be able to support yourself financially.

People with advanced degrees from their native country in areas such as medicine or engineering may need U.S. recertification before being allowed to practice their profession in the United States. This process can be expensive and take a long time. It requires proof of education and qualification in the individual's native country, and also qualifying scores on English language tests. Refugees seeking to reenter their professions frequently take a less specialized job in their field while they prepare for recertification. For example, a doctor may work as a laboratory assistant before becoming recertified.

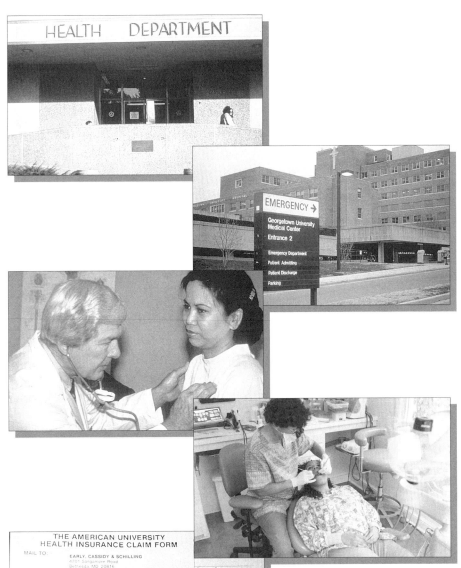

THE AMERICAN UNIVERSITY
HEALTH INSURANCE CLAIM FORM

MAIL TO: EARLY, CASSIDY & SCHILLING
              4701 Sangamore Road
              Bethesda, MD 20816
              (301) 229-3400   Coverage Code

Policy Number   — TO BE COMPLETED BY STUDENT? —   Social Security No.

Student's Name _____ _____   Age ____
                First Name   First Name

Present Address _____ _____ _____ ____
                No. and Street   City or Town   State   Zip

Home Address _____ _____ _____ ____
                No. and Street   City or Town   State   Zip

If claim for dependent, give name and relationship

Date of accident or illness

Nature of injury or illness

If injury, describe fully how and
where accident occurred

If injured in play or practice of sport,
indicate what sport

RETURNED IF NOT FULLY COMPLETED

Your first contact with U.S. health care will probably be at your initial health screening. Your resettlement agency will arrange for this screening soon after you arrive. The screening will identify and treat any health problems that may interfere with your resettlement, such as your ability to work or your children's ability to go to school. Your children will receive immunizations during the screening because all children enrolling in public school must show proof that they have been immunized. The health screening is free of charge and is usually done at a public health clinic, a community health center, or a doctor's office.

After the initial health screening, you will need to figure out how you will get health care when you or a member of your family needs it. To do that you will need to understand how Americans think about health and how the U.S. health care system works.

American Concepts of Health

Americans believe that illness can be prevented through cleanliness, proper nutrition, exercise, and adequate sleep. They wear clothing that keeps them warm in cold weather and clothing that helps them stay cool in hot weather. They go to the doctor or clinic once a year for a checkup, so that they will know about any health problems before they become serious. They go to the dentist to have their teeth cleaned. They call all of this maintaining a healthy lifestyle.

The U.S. health care system relies heavily on scientific methods to diagnose and treat patients. This means that, in addition to asking patients how they feel, doctors often do tests, using blood or other physical samples. The results of the tests help the doctor decide how to

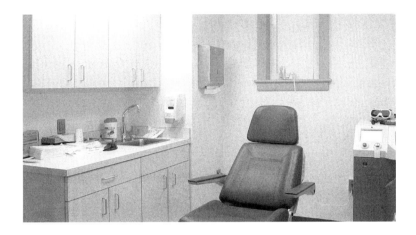

treat the patient. If you are uncomfortable having blood drawn or giving other samples, talk with your doctor about it.

Doctors in the United States are not always familiar with ways of treating illness in other countries. You may need to explain to your doctor how you or your children have been treated in the past, and describe the practices or remedies you commonly use to respond to illness.

Health Care Providers

There are several different types of health care providers in the United States. The staff at your resettlement agency can tell you which types of providers are in your community and what services they offer.

Public health department. Each state has a public health department with offices in communities throughout the state. Public health departments provide immunizations against diseases and offer other preventive health services, including testing and treatment for tuberculosis. For refugees, these services are free or very inexpensive.

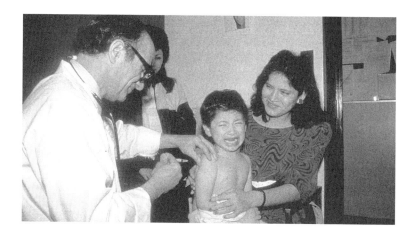

Community clinics and health centers. These provide basic health services and health counseling. Some also provide dental care and eye examinations. Some clinics in cities treat specific types of patients, such as pregnant women or people with HIV/AIDS. Clinics accept private insurance and Medicaid, and many charge fees based on the patient's ability to pay. Patients usually need to make an appointment to visit the clinic, although some clinics will take people on a walk-in basis.

Private doctors. Some doctors are general practitioners who provide general health care, including annual checkups. Others specialize in one area of medicine. Some doctors work as part of a private clinic or in a group with other general practitioners and specialists. A patient must make an appointment to see a doctor. The doctor's office usually requires proof of ability to pay or insurance information at the time of the appointment.

Private dentists. Some dentists provide general dental care, including cleanings and fillings. Others spe-

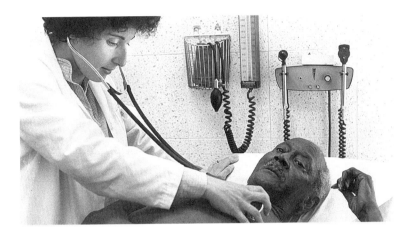

cialize in specific types of dental problems. Dentists' offices require payment at the time of the appointment. Health insurance does not always cover dental care.

Pharmacies. These are stores where you can obtain medications prescribed by your doctor, and also non-prescription medications such as pain relievers. The pharmacist can advise you about what medications to use for your illness and whether you can take certain medications in combination with others. You must pay or provide insurance information when you receive your prescription from the pharmacist.

Hospitals. Doctors and clinics refer patients with special problems to the hospital for tests and surgery. Hospital care is expensive, and hospitals require proof of insurance or ability to pay for those services.

Emergency rooms. These facilities in hospitals or elsewhere are for sudden, extreme health problems. You do not need an appointment to go to the emergency room, but they are busy places and you will have to wait a long time if your problem is not serious. If your problem is not an emergency, you should make an appointment at a clinic or doctor's office. Emergency room care is very expensive.

Ambulance service. This service provides medical help and transportation to an emergency room when there is no other way to take the injured or sick person to receive emergency medical care. Ambulance services charge a fee after service has been provided.

Mental Health Care

Americans believe that mental health is as important as physical health, and health care includes treatment by a mental health professional when necessary. Refugees and other newcomers need to pay special attention to their mental health because they often have experienced trauma during their flight and great stress as they adjust to life in the United States. If you ever feel so overwhelmed by your situation that you cannot cope with everyday activities, you should seek mental health services. Most mental health care is provided through clinics, private doctors and therapists, but some mental health services are also available through MAAs and social service agencies. Some resettlement agencies also provide counseling, support groups, or life skills groups, and they can help you find other mental health services.

Paying for Health Care

Health care in the United States is expensive, and individuals, not the government, are responsible for paying for health services. The cost of health care is high, so most people rely on insurance programs. Many employers offer insurance programs for their employees, and they often pay part of the monthly cost. The rest is deducted from your paycheck along with your taxes, so you do not have to make an additional payment. There is usually a waiting period from the time you are hired until you become eligible for health insurance.

Employers often provide health insurance through a health maintenance organization (HMO) or a preferred provider organization (PPO). With these, a group of private doctors and clinics provides care. Each participant (that is, each employee) is assigned a doctor. This doctor treats the participant and must approve any visits to emergency rooms, hospitals, or specialists. In some situations, the HMO or PPO pays the full cost of health care he or she receives. In other situations the participant must pay part of the cost.

If your employer does not offer health benefits, you can purchase health insurance directly from an insurance company, HMO, or PPO. Staff at your resettlement agency can advise you on how to do this.

To assist people with low incomes, there are government programs that pay for some medical care. Refugees are eligible to apply for Refugee Medical Assistance (RMA) or Medicaid. Both programs pay for medical care for working-age people with low incomes, but they are meant to be used only until you can get insurance through an employer or on your own. To apply for these programs, you must complete forms that provide proof of your income and other personal information. Eligibility is frequently checked and updated. Many doctors do not accept these forms of insurance.

Refugees over the age of 65 are eligible for Medicare. This is a federal program that helps people over the age of 65 with their medical expenses. Medicare also covers part of the cost of prescription medication.

Your resettlement agency can help you understand the medical assistance available to you.

Your Health Care Rights

Wherever in the United States you live, you have the right to interpreter services and to confidentiality.

Interpreter services. You need to be able to understand and communicate with your doctor so you can receive the right treatment. If you feel you need language assistance to communicate with your doctor, you have the right to have an interpreter help you. Ask your resettlement agency for help in finding an interpreter.

Confidentiality. Everything that takes place between you and your doctor is confidential under the law. Your doctor cannot tell your family, your friends, or your employer about your health situation without your consent. This includes information about serious conditions such as HIV. If you are HIV positive or have another medical illness, you are the one to decide whether to tell your family and friends. The doctor cannot tell them unless you agree. But the law requires you to inform your doctor of your HIV positive status. If you do not, you could face serious penalties.

The cost of living in the United States is very high. You will need to be careful with your money, so that you do not spend more than you can afford. The staff at your resettlement agency can help you make a budget, so that you will know how much money you have, how much you can spend, and how much you can save.

Planning for Expenses

Every month you will need to pay for your basic living costs and other expenses. These will be your major living costs:

Rent. This will probably be your largest expense every month.

Utilities. Utilities include electricity, gas or oil, water, and trash collection. Some of these may be included in your rent, but you may have to pay for one or more separately. Your bills for electricity and gas or oil will be higher in the winter and summer months when you need more heat or more air conditioning.

Food. You can save money on food by looking for the stores and products with the lowest prices.

Child care. Child care may be a large expense every month. If you cannot arrange child care with a family member or friend, your resettlement agency may be able to help you find child care or apply for childcare assistance.

Transportation. This will include the cost of travel to and from work, stores, and appointments. In many places, monthly discount passes for buses or subways are available.

" *A few years after I came to the United States, I decided it was time to buy a car. When I applied for a loan from the car dealer, the loan officer asked me if I had ever taken out a loan before.*

I said I had and showed him the IOM loan that I had paid off. Because I showed that I could pay off the loan, my loan application was approved. "

Telephone. You will need to pay for your telephone every month. Remember that long distance calls to other countries can be expensive.

Travel loan. You will need to make payments on your travel loan every month until you have repaid it all.

Savings and support for your family overseas. If you have long-range goals such as education or buying a home, you may want to put an amount into a savings account every month. You may also want to send money to family members who are still in your home country. When you have a job and know how much your monthly expenses will be, you can decide how much you can save or send home each month.

Health care. Once you have a full-time job, you may be offered some form of health insurance. However, many entry-level jobs do not offer insurance for the first months of employment. You may need to purchase your own insurance.

Where to Shop

Stores and markets in the United States offer many different kinds of goods and services. Here are five types of places to shop:

Supermarkets. These are the most common types of food store. Most also sell cleaning products, cosmetics, magazines, household items, and nonprescription drugs. Many people reduce food costs by using discount coupons and purchasing supermarket store brands or brands that are on sale.

Department stores. These sell furniture, appliances, hardware, clothing, shoes, and other nonfood items. Some are discount stores, where prices are lower.

Thrift shops. These sell used items, including furniture, household items, and clothing, at reduced prices.

Ethnic food stores. These are often owned and managed by immigrants or former refugees. They may be found wherever a large immigrant population is living. You may find familiar foods from your homeland in an ethnic food store.

Yard sales and garage sales. At these sales, people sell items from their homes, usually at very low prices. They are excellent places to buy household items, furniture, and clothing. Yard and garage sales are advertised in the newspaper or on signs in the neighborhood.

Paying Taxes
Taxes in the United States pay for many of the services used by all residents, including refugees. Taxes pay for

public education, maintenance of roads and highways, police, fire, and emergency services, and social service programs. People living in the United States pay three kinds of taxes:

Income taxes. Every working person pays federal income tax, and residents of some states also pay a state income tax. These are withheld from your pay-check by your employer. Each year you must file tax return forms with the federal and state governments. These forms tell the government how much you paid in taxes through your employer's withholding, and whether you owe tax or whether you you will get a refund from the government. Your resettlement agency can help you get tax return forms and advise you about filing them. These forms must be sent to the government by April 15 each year.

Personal property taxes. Local governments collect property taxes on homes, land, and buildings that you own. Some places also collect property taxes on auto-mobiles.

Sales taxes. Consumers in most states pay a sales tax in addition to the cost of the item. For some items, such as food or medicine, there might not be a tax. This tax is a percentage of the cost of the item and is calculated at the cash register. The price given on an item or on the store shelf usually does not include the sales tax.

Banking
To keep their money safe, Americans often keep it in an account at a bank or credit union, rather than at home or with them. Money that you put in a bank is insured by

the U.S. government. If the money is lost or stolen, the U.S. government will pay it back to you.

Banks have different kinds of accounts for different purposes. Banks charge a monthly fee for some of these accounts. There are two main types of bank accounts:

Savings accounts and money market accounts. These are for saving money. Banks pay you interest on these accounts in exchange for keeping your money.

Checking accounts. These are for paying expenses. The bank gives you checks that you can fill out to pay your rent and other bills. You must be careful not to write checks for more money than you have in your checking account. Some banks also pay interest on some checking accounts.

Using Credit and Establishing a Good Credit History

Americans commonly use credit cards and credit plans for major purchases such as cars, appliances, and furniture. With credit cards and credit plans, people can buy expensive things, because they can make several small payments over time instead of one large payment at the time of purchase.

When you use a credit plan or credit card, you are borrowing money. The bank or company that issues the card charges interest on the amount you owe, and you must make a payment every month. If you miss a payment, the company can take back the product you bought with credit and charge you a fee.

If you decide to get a credit card, you should use it very carefully. It is very easy to get deeply into debt using credit cards. Before you purchase something on credit, be sure that you are going to be able to make the monthly payment.

When you have loans or use credit, you establish your credit history. Private credit reporting agencies keep a credit report that shows your credit history, and banks look at this when you ask for a loan or a credit card. If you make your payments on time every month, your credit history will be good and banks will be willing to lend you money and issue credit cards. If you miss your payments or charge more on your credit cards than you can afford to pay back, you will have a bad credit history and you will not be able to obtain loans or credit in the future.

For this reason, you need to set aside money to repay your travel loan every month. It is your first chance to establish a good credit history in the United States. It is much easier to get a loan in the future if you can show that you have repaid a loan in the past. Ask your resettlement agency for information about how to repay your travel loan.

You also need to pay your rent and utility bills on time every month. If you fall behind in your payments, the utility company can take legal action against you through a collection agency. This action will also appear on your credit report.

Laws in the United States are intended to protect your rights. As a resident of the United States, you should have a basic knowledge of your legal rights and responsibilities.

Your Rights

As a refugee, you have the same rights as everyone else living in the United States. These rights include freedom of speech, freedom of religion, and freedom of assembly. You cannot be arrested or imprisoned for expressing an opinion, practicing your religion, or meeting with a group of your friends. You should feel free to worship, dress, and conduct your daily activities as you please as long as you obey U.S. and local laws.

All residents of the United States are entitled to equal protection of their rights in employment, housing, education, and eligibility for government services. U.S. law also prohibits discrimination on the basis of race, religion, or ethnic background. Although some recent events have caused great fear, sadness, and anger among Americans, most Americans are not prejudiced against immigrants or refugees. This is because most Americans have ancestors who were immigrants or refugees. However, there are some Americans who hold a negative opinion about people who have come to the United States from other countries. If you are discriminated against or denied your rights because of your appearance or the language you speak, you have the right to police protection and to seek legal action. Legal assistance services are available in many communities. Your resettlement agency can help you find them.

If you are accused of a crime in the United States, you are considered innocent until you are proven guilty. You

have the right to a lawyer who will represent you in court. If you cannot afford a lawyer, the court will pay for one to represent you. However, if you break the law, your resettlement agency cannot intervene for you.

Your Responsibilities

There are three kinds of laws in the United States. Federal laws, such as the laws against drug trafficking, apply to every person living in the United States. State laws vary by state; for example, in some states you can get a driver's license at age 16, but in others you must be 18. Local laws apply in a particular city or county. You need to understand U.S. laws because many of them differ from the laws in your home country.

In the United States, you can be punished if you break the law, even if you did not know about the law you broke. As a refugee, you need to remember that the penalty for some offenses is deportation (return) to your home country. Ask your resettlement agency if you have questions about any of these laws.

Here are a few important things you should know about U.S. laws:

- It is illegal to purchase, sell, or use narcotics or other addictive drugs and controlled substances. If you break this law, you can be sent back to your home country. You should check with your resettlement agency to learn whether drugs that are legal in your home country are controlled or illegal in the United States.

- It is illegal to physically abuse (hit or beat) your spouse or child. It is also illegal to leave children without adult supervision. In some countries, it is the custom for older children to take care of younger children, but in the United States, young children must be supervised by an adult. Beating a child is considered abuse, and leaving a child unattended is considered neglect. Both of these offenses can lead to the removal of your children by a child protection agency.

- Sex with minors (under 18 years of age in most states) is illegal. Sexual abuse of a minor can lead to imprisonment and deportation. Marriage to more than one spouse (polygamy) is also illegal.

- If you have children and become divorced or legally separated from your spouse, you must continue to provide financial support for your children through regular payments to your former spouse. This is called child support, and it is a legal obligation. Failure to provide child support can jeopardize your immigration status.

- Children in the United States may not drink alcohol until they reach the age of 21, and children may not buy liquor in stores. In general, it is also illegal to drink alcoholic beverages on the street or outdoors, except in designated areas such as bars or restaurants.

- Offensive comments or behavior of a sexual nature in the workplace (sexual harassment) is illegal.

- It is illegal to own firearms without a license. In most places, it is also illegal to hunt game or fish without a license, and you must learn and obey other laws relating to natural resources.

- It is illegal to drive a car if you do not have a U.S. driver's license or if you have been drinking alcohol. Driving while under the influence of alcohol (DUI) is considered very serious and can lead to the loss of your driver's license, imprisonment, and possibly deportation.

- Many states have laws regarding the use of seatbelts in automobiles. Parents are required to use seatbelts for children and special safety seats for infants. There are similar seatbelt laws for adults.

- It is illegal to smoke in public places such as theaters or offices. In other places, such as restaurants, there may be a special area for smoking. If you smoke, ask your resettlement agency about the laws in your area.

- There are laws protecting treatment of animals in the United States. It is illegal to beat, neglect, abuse, or sacrifice an animal.

Your Legal Status and Citizenship

Resettlement is a permanent decision for most refugees. Admission as a refugee allows you to reside permanently in the United States and eventually to apply for citizenship.

For your first year in the United States, you will be in refugee status. During this time you should carry a copy of your I-94 and your EAD card with you at all times as proof of your legal status. As a refugee, you can do the following:

- Travel anywhere within the United States

- Buy property

- Be employed

- Attend school

- Sponsor your spouse and unmarried children under 21 years of age if you have been separated from them because of flight from your country of origin. If you wish to have your spouse or children join you in the United States, your resettlement agency will explain the requirements and procedures to you.

While you hold refugee status, you cannot obtain a U.S. passport, join the military, vote in elections, or be employed in government jobs that require U.S. citizenship. Also, although you can travel anywhere within the United States, you must tell USCIS if you move. You are required to notify USCIS within 10 days of changing your address. Your resettlement agency can help you fill out the necessary form.

While you hold refugee status, you may not travel outside the United States without permission from USCIS. If you must travel overseas, your resettlement agency will explain how to request permission. If you return to your country of origin while you are a refugee, you might not be permitted to reenter the United States.

Male refugees between the ages of 18 and 25 must register with the Selective Service, a government agency that can call individuals for military service, usually in time of war. At present, all members of the U.S. military are volunteers. People who do not register might find it difficult to get permanent residency and citizenship.

After 1 year in the United States, you can apply to become a permanent resident. Permanent residents can travel overseas (although they should not stay abroad for more than 1 year) and can be members of the U.S. military, but they cannot vote in U.S. elections or hold U.S.

government jobs that require citizenship. Your resettlement agency will explain how to become a permanent resident.

After 4 years and 9 months in the United States, you can apply for citizenship. USCIS or your resettlement agency can explain the requirements for citizenship. Among them are a good moral character and a basic knowledge of English and of U.S. history and government. Naturalized citizens enjoy the same rights and privileges as citizens born in the United States.

The United States is a nation of immigrants who brought with them many different cultural traditions and practices, so there is no single American culture. However, Americans do accept and expect certain standards of behavior. These may be different from those of your own culture, and they may seem strange or even contradict some of the accepted behaviors in your country. You will be more successful in the United States if you are observant, flexible, and open to change, and if you are willing to ask questions about behavior that puzzles you. Here are some things you should know about American values, attitudes, and behavior:

Informality. Americans tend to be more informal than most other people. In social situations, they usually use first names. In business situations, last names are used before a formal introduction has taken place, but many supervisors and most coworkers may prefer to use first names. Professional titles such as Doctor are usually used only in formal situations. Americans smile a lot, and use a smile when greeting both friends and strangers.

Punctuality. Clock time is highly valued. Americans try to be punctual and expect others to be punctual, too. Making and keeping appointments is necessary in private and public life. If you do not make an appointment before visiting a business office, you might not be seen, and if you cannot keep an appointment or you expect to be more than 15 minutes late, you should call, explain that you will be late, and apologize.

Privacy. Americans place a high value on personal privacy. People seldom visit each other's homes without calling ahead or being invited first. Financial matters are considered private, and it is considered impolite to ask

how much someone earns or what he paid for his house or car. It is also considered impolite to ask personal questions of someone you do not know or have just met.

Personal hygiene. Most Americans bathe or shower everyday, brush their teeth and shampoo their hair often, and wash their clothes frequently. Stores sell many kinds of cleaning products that help people avoid appearing dirty or having any odor of sweat. Personal hygiene can be especially important for getting and keeping a job, both in the interview and on the job. Ask your resettlement agency for more information about this.

Tipping. It is customary to give a tip of 15% or 20% of the bill to a waiter in a restaurant or to a taxi driver. You should not give money or tips to a police officer or any government official as thanks for assistance.

Alcohol and smoking. Although alcohol is consumed in the United States, there are many laws governing its use and sale. The decision whether to drink alcohol is considered a personal choice, and it is never impolite to refuse a drink in the United States. Many Americans do

not smoke, and they may expect others to refrain from smoking in their homes.

Personal safety. Although crime and violence exist in the United States, the amount of crime differs in different parts of the country. No matter where you live, you should take basic precautions, such as locking your home and car, never carrying large amounts of cash with you, and knowing which neighborhoods to avoid at night.

Personal identification. Because the U.S. population is so large, Americans use standardized forms of identification in their dealings with government and business. You should always carry a copy of your I-94 card and your EAD card, as well as the name, address, and phone number of your resettlement agency. If you do not speak English, carry your own telephone number and address, or the address and telephone number of anyone you are about to visit.

The process of learning about American behaviors and values and coping with them is part of cultural adjustment. Making this adjustment does not mean you have

to give up all aspects of your own cultural identity. In fact, most refugees feel that they have successfully adjusted when they have learned to integrate aspects of American culture with some of their own.

Coping with Culture Shock and Stress

Culture shock includes feelings of being helpless or frustrated in a country where you do not speak the language or understand the culture. Culture shock is normal; anyone going to live in a new country can experience it.

If you are experiencing culture shock, you may feel

- frustrated at not being able to accomplish daily tasks such as shopping or taking public transportation;
- tired during the day or unable to sleep well;
- angry or irritable;
- indifferent or sad; and,
- uninterested in eating.

The move to a new and strange country is stressful for most refugees. Everyone experiences this kind of stress differently, but there are some common feelings that you may recognize in yourself, such as a lack of motivation, lack of self-confidence, loss of a sense of identity, and disappointment. These feelings are usually temporary and diminish over time. Many newcomers to the United States have experienced these feelings and have become stronger and more capable as they dealt with them.

Sometimes this stress can lead to difficulties handling everyday life, family conflict, and even domestic violence. It is important for you to recognize the stress you are feeling, locate resources, and develop coping skills.

Ways to cope with culture shock vary among cultures and individuals. You may already have developed some coping skills, such as eating well, exercising, and getting enough sleep; getting together with friends or attending a social or cultural event; setting personal goals; and contacting religious or spiritual resources such as your local mosque, church or synagogue. Some people feel better when they can enjoy a favorite activity or listen to familiar music. One strategy used by nearly all newcomers is to join groups such as mutual assistance associations formed by and for people from their particular nationality or ethnic group.

Ask your resettlement agency for assistance in any of these areas.

Changing Roles Within the Family

One of the most stressful aspects of resettlement is the change in family roles. Fathers, mothers, teenagers, young children, and the elderly all find that life in the United States can change their relationships with one another. This is a normal part of resettlement, but it can create difficulties at first.

Both men and women may have difficulty adjusting to the roles of men and women in the United States. Americans believe in equality of the sexes and value self-sufficiency and independence for both men and women. In many families, both the husband and the wife work, and they share child care responsibilities.

In some families, when both parents are working, the wife earns more than the husband. In other families, the wife has found a job and the husband has not. In this case, the husband will be expected to care for the children when they are not in school. In situations like these, refugee men often feel a loss of their leadership role in the family. Refugee women may feel a newfound confidence but also a sense of guilt.

Resettlement can be very difficult for young people, especially teenagers, because they must adjust to life in a new culture at the same time they are expected to maintain the traditional way of life at home and in their communities. And they must do this at a time when they are facing changes as they grow from adolescence to young adulthood.

Because they often learn English faster than their parents, young people may be asked to act as interpreters for their parents and take on other new responsibilities. Often they must both go to school and hold a job. Their parents can feel unable to help them because of their own limited understanding of the U.S. school system. And teens often feel they cannot communicate the stress they feel to their parents.

When these stresses become too great, some young people turn to harmful behaviors, such as being absent from school, joining a gang, or using drugs. These behaviors can lead to more problems because they are illegal. For unmarried girls, harmful behaviors can lead to pregnancy.

Changing roles are also stressful for the elderly, who may feel that they have lost their former status as sources of knowledge and experience in the family. In the United States, the emphasis on youth and productivity can make the elderly feel ignored and useless. The difficulties of learning a new language and a new culture can lead to feelings of isolation and loneliness. The elderly may find that they no longer hold a position of respect in their society.

The economic challenges of being an elderly refugee can also be overwhelming. Some older refugees who expected to retire and receive a pension may find themselves in need of employment, especially if they are under age 65. Refugees over 65 may discover that U.S. retirement benefits are not what they expected, that disability benefits do not cover their medical expenses, and/or that their families cannot support them as they may have in their home countries. These economic challenges, together with the loss of status and sense of isolation, can lead to depression and other mental health issues.

If you or a member of your family ever feel unable to cope with the stress of your new life in the United States, seek help immediately. Issues about new family roles should be openly discussed in Cultural Orientation classes or with your caseworker in the United States. Your resettlement agency can locate resources to help you develop coping skills and to improve stressful situations at home.

Resettlement is a long process. You may need from 2 to 5 years to adjust fully to life in your new community. Try to be observant and nonjudgmental, and set goals for yourself. Honest communication, patience, and a cooperative attitude toward those trying to help will help greatly in your adjustment. It will also help to understand basic American values, such as self-reliance and independence. Discovering a new culture is challenging, but it can also be enriching and fulfilling.

" My feelings about this country are now very different from when I first came here. When I was in Vietnam, I thought coming to America was like heaven or something. That's what people were telling me. Now, I don't imagine it's like a heaven. It's just better than Vietnam. "

" Although we are living in America, we still have the right to remember and keep our traditions. We still learn about American lives and customs. We still copy and follow some of them, but at the same time we have to know that although we don't have our own country, we still remember, recognize and treasure our culture. Welcome to all of you who are to come here. "

" You cannot learn everything about this life in two months. It takes years and years. "

" I have changed in the past year. I don't feel so homesick now as I was in the beginning and I'm not afraid of new things anymore. I learned how to get a better job by learning English. "

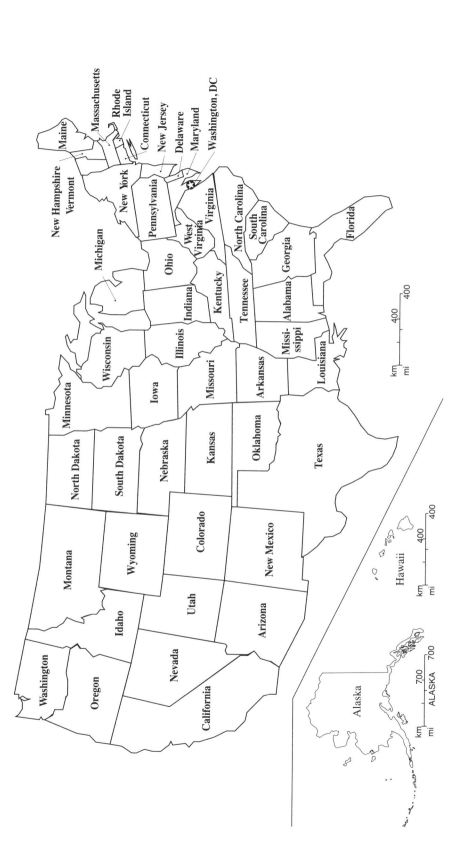